Acclaim for the Writing of Nick Purdon

"Nick's musings of his own journey depict the darkness of the soul and enlightenment. Through his words we are able to observe the life of a man in deep reflection and consider his journey while contemplating our own life's route."
        Irene Watson, author of *The Sitting Swing* and *Rewriting Life Scripts*

"*The Road-Shaped Heart* by Nick Purdon will squeeze the heart of each reader to elicit emotions held tight. Each reader will find their own life pain and loss within the words spread before them like a feast to be swallowed until the soul has been touched. With passages such as, '…my boots choke back tears of wet streets and the last grains of hope become trapped in their grooves' and 'I can only turn my face slowly like a sunflower/To the east where the sun forgot to rise' one is filled with visions and a sense of knowingness. Read *The Road-Shaped Heart*, then close its cover—your heart will open, your soul will thank you."
        Barbara Sinor, Ph.D., author
        Tales of Addiction and Inspiration for Recovery

"Nick Purdon pits the fragility of the human heart against god-like forces, but not with violence. He does it with a quiet acceptance of the vulnerability of the pulpy, red smallness at the pumping core of us. The enormity of a bewilderingly cruel world of thoughtless gods who disrupt our lives the way a child disrupts a line of ants, highlights, rather than diminishes, the determination of our industrious selves to make sense of life, with all its burrs and thorns, its freesias, sunflowers and roses. And with our almost incorporeal hearts that beat bloodily, despairingly, and ironically, always hopefully, at the centre of things."
        Karin Schimke, *Cape Times*

[Karin Schimke is a widely published journalist, columnist, author and poet, and MC of the long-run weekly Cape Town poetry event *Off The Wall*.]

The Road-Shaped Heart

Nick Purdon

Cover Art and Illustrations by Felicity Purdon

World Voices Series

Modern History Press

The Road-Shaped Heart
Copyright © 2011 by Nick Purdon. All Rights Reserved.
Cover art and illustrations by Felicity Purdon
From the World Voices Series

Library of Congress Cataloging-in-Publication Data

Purdon, Nick, 1976-
  The road-shaped heart : poems / by Nick Purdon ; cover art and illustrations by Felicity Purdon ; foreword by Sherry Quan Lee.
      p. cm. -- (World voices)
  ISBN-13: 978-1-61599-056-6 (hardcover : alk. paper)
  ISBN-10: 1-61599-056-9 (hardcover : alk. paper)
  ISBN-13: 978-1-61599-057-3 (trade pbk. : alk. paper)
  ISBN-10: 1-61599-057-7 (trade pbk. : alk. paper)
  I. Purdon, Felicity. II. Title.
  PR9369.4.P87R63 2011
  821'.92--dc22
                              2011007843

Published by
Modern History Press, an imprint of Loving Healing Press
5145 Pontiac Trail
Ann Arbor, MI 48105

www.ModernHistoryPress.com
FAX 734-663-6861
Tollfree 888-761-6268

Distributed by
Ingram Book Group, Bertram's Books (UK)

*To Dad: for all your support
and for
Mom: no longer with us, but always with us.*

"I dare not linger, for my long walk has not yet ended."
—Nelson Mandela, *Long Walk to Freedom*

Contents

Acknowledgments	2
Foreword by Sherry Quan Lee	3
Introduction	4
Table for One	5
Roses Amongst a December of Thorns	6
Glint	7
Leaving Port	8
Poseidon's Waters	9
Lethe	9
Siren	11
Withdrawal	13
Delirium Tremens	15
Gothic Woman	16
Lithium Carbonate	17
Burrs	18
Concentricity	19
Sheath	21
The Offering (under Thunderwood skies)	23
A Sunday Afternoon	25
Softly, softly	26
And, I Will	27
On Saying Goodbye	28
Walls	29
Husk	31
Detonation Alley	32
Birthday	33
Shock, decoded	35
Scattering Your Ashes at Kalk Bay	37
About the Author	38

Acknowledgments

Thank you to my publisher, Victor R. Volkman, for giving an unknown author the opportunity to realize a dream and for all the speedy responses to my many questions.

To my editor, Sherry Quan Lee, my heartfelt thanks for all your honest critiques and insights and for drawing the best out of me and my writing.

Thank you also to my sister, Felicity Purdon, for the inspirational cover design and illustrations.

Foreword by Sherry Quan Lee

Nick Purdon's manuscript of poems is an intimate journey of self-reflection. His poetic voice is natural, metaphoric, clear and concise. His poems, though personal are universal. Nick is a keen observer of not only his own life, but of the lives of others who have entered, though perhaps are no longer part of, his journey. He observes, but he doesn't judge.

Nick's poems, though often melancholy, are sensitive, sincere, and skillful. The poems present a man with conviction, trust, strength—and love. The poems also present a man who loves language, and loves story (myths and legends). He owns words that are tough and tender, and words that are candid and shrewd.

Although Nick is from South Africa and I am from Midwestern U.S.A., as a woman and a writer, I connect with Nick's poems on many levels through my own historical experiential lens. My favorite poems are *Glint*, *Withdrawal*, *Delirium Tremens*, *Lithium Carbonate*, *Walls*, *Softly, softly*, and *Scattering Your Ashes at Kalk Bay*.

As you read *The Road-Shaped Heart* you will enter and be immersed with Nick Purdon's journey which will surely elicit your own.

Sherry Quan Lee is the author of *Chinese Blackbird*, and *How to Write a Suicide Note: serial essays that saved a woman's life* from Modern History Press.

Introduction

Being a poet means more to me than simply writing poems. It means embracing the life that fate has laid down for me with passion, intensity and nobility. It means embracing all the joys and sorrows of the human experience to the absolute fullest. Though the lens through which my experiences are viewed is particular to me, the experiences themselves are common to most people. From the euphoria of falling in love to the sorrow of death and every emotion in between, I seek to give these experiences a voice. Or rather I am compelled to, even though I don't always understand why. Sometimes it feels almost a little arrogant to presume that I was chosen to be a voice to articulate a feeling or an experience. Poetry is about touching someone else intimately and it is, for me anyway, somehow always reciprocal. I don't just want to make you, the reader, think. I want you to feel.

The Road-Shaped Heart is about a journey through darkness, anguish, addiction, loss and grief into hope, faith and self-forgiveness. The poems were written between 2003 and 2010. I hope that you will find much that you, too, can relate to. Ultimately it is about always staying loyal and faithful to our journey, to the paths in life we take that shape our hearts.

Table for One

The girl in pink wants another balloon
The blue one has drifted out of the window
With her parents' deflated conversation
Her mother sighs: "There is nothing left *to* save."
Her father shakes his head, spears his heart
With his fork. The wind reaches in through the window and snatches them
like a Griffin and drops them separately on two distant tors
They have balled up like armadillos.

I draw deeply on the remaining half-inch of my cigarette
and kill it like the rest.
I wonder the same yellowed thought:
 Is a single tendril of smoke ultimately less pained?
A beer arrives. I thank the waitress in a voice carved out by distant glaciers.

Roses Amongst a December of Thorns

December's thorns
Tear my hand; my crimson
Grip stains these
White-knuckle days

I will not accept this flower's touch:
The finest china of a terrible sadness
Crushed to powder it leaves shards
Rendering palms unreadable, unbelievable.

A glide of knives on twisted stems:
Dead stars to holly-hook my flesh.
A sweet scent has turned astringent
A vase of roses left on a bedside table –

Twelve bruised eyes pool in a fractured mirror.

Glint

Oh this *is* quick, so steely sharp
It is a scalpel, be cautious when you wield it
Taken to our polarities
It will shave the dead wood; bone chips

Will fall away, the way your worldly costume
Coyly slides off bare shoulders and nape
And spirit slips down around your ankles.
I wore a halo of innocence –

You knocked it off in haste, it
Clattered to the floor.
White-coat knife-thrower, *you should know*:

This heart was not designed to be dissected
And pinned to a pitted specimen tray beside the weak
Frowned upon and poked by unskilled fingers

A disposable carcass, the fat red pump removed.
I sit on your shelf in a musty room:
A bag of nerves in a jar of alcohol.

Leaving Port

There is a sense of coolness
In my disappearance over the horizon
These are mine: distilled crystals of coldness
I scatter them beneath the polar sun
Into which I have sailed.

Heavy, like a spell about to break,
I try to drop anchor
But can only circumnavigate like clockwork
Grinding grudgingly back to the same old place
So fierce, these teeth bite the hardest.

Open eyes as white as sails
The cracked compass deceives –
My needle spinning in the squalls,
I flirt with, but never touch,
The harbour lights.

Out in the sea, a glimpse of a buoy
In the deep, churning waves
Blown to black, a bruising back
And, like *The Flying Dutchman,*
This, too, will be my fate.

Poseidon's Waters

Thundering sea god splits the night
his hands, claws of rain,
become familiar songs scratching
against stained panes of a glass vice.

Impaled on his trident
my ant-body
separates like oil and water.
Taken to the flame

I curl like a singed strand of hair,
the fingers of conch wombs let me go,
let me dilate in the wind.
Hot sand melts me crystal clear and the ache is gone -

my welt-red newborn memories gasp in the dark for air.

Lethe

stoned
i awoke, cold
as slab
just
a rustle
in the rest.
Closed.

Siren

From atoll to atoll step
carefully so close to the edges
(But I know you've heard me calling)

Within her song the feathered lure hides
its barbed hook the open-mouthed wait
She cannot love me though her honey

strips flesh from bone and unclothes
the insatiable threads of mortal tastes
Disguised, she is the scarlet

retinal splash that unblinds
and uncolours a world in negative
Polarized skies lower with my mind

at the abyss edge to where all water
must flow – compelling, imploring:
Her voice catches in my chest

Here we are inextricably bound
in whispers, where truths hurry after secrets:
(Tell me what you've never told another)

I Gather them from stone smoothed
by her waters, in a soporific lungful of her voice
(Mine, mine, entwined minds of sweet Somniferum)

She is in my skin, wearing my skin as I
smother under the covers of her carbonous clouds
with doors that close, my eyes that close

(Sleep here... sleep beside me...)

Withdrawal

As the dark clouds roll in,
heaving, they bring

decaying ravens plummeting
from a sky of cracked bones.

Black spears of Lethe pierce
and tear my eyes from their sockets,

nerve-whole with dull blue irises
that stare round as blank as silence.

Blood thickened with ice,
an itch of splintered glass

strips my body parts
and places each on twenty-eight

stakes, where scavengers perch
and gorge themselves hungrily.

Delirium Tremens

White noise sandblasts midnight into my eyes

Cleanse the air of spiders, flowers and floaters
Replace bilious cracks with descending dry mouthed cries
and the room with shadows that loom at the foot of sleep

Pulling, tugging –

Follow the trail of spinning constellations, I am in a frenzy

Smoky barrel; a bullet morning
           crystals of consciousness, a lilting requiem reopens
                  the wound of the night,
bleeding like belladonna, panic!
         heave in the shock

The shaking of heads in disbelief,
the headless in their defeat wonder
at the sight of the one with bruised bones

A gathering of ants around death

In a shroud of cold sweat
           the ugly sister of joy appears,
                hands gnarled
against a gloaming sky, mirror after mirror
           bounces the same image in a crumbling sleep
                as hard to attain as not

        In that mind sky the sun bursts like a poppy, a thousand children
stillborn in the eye of a tremor but blown restless

A scattering of discarded husks swirl in gales

I cannot hold onto this breath any longer

        So let my body fall like a burning cross into blinding synesthesia.

Gothic Woman

The pregnant sky drifted slowly above us like a jellyfish
Tentacles stinging that April evening
With the early arrival of winter
Blood-spots of rain dampened your long coat
From the inside out, bleeding from
The ineffable burr of sorrow that lodged itself in your throat

I saw the sleepy red eye of your wound open slowly
You opened the door a crack
Such was the godless gale that grieved through your canyons
That it whipped you crypt-still and stinging raw
Crouched in a corner, your hands wrung out the shadows
Cast by your falling chin on the hardness of Hell's knees
A place where the taste of your angel's desertion
Remained acrid on your tongue

From the flowering thunder of trees that forested your days
Beneath the nights' silver lancets that sliced up your heart
You hung
And the endured atrocities you whispered
Hung and snapped my neck from your dark boughs
You spilled thick from my eyes, like tar down to my feet
Rooted, as one by one
Confessions, like flesh stripped from the bones of innocence
Trailed unwaveringly from you like a wolf's aria

Your hands reached out to me
But I too was imprisoned and unable to rescue you
Pinned amongst my own blackthorns like a shrike's prey
I could only watch you draw in the world around you
And steadily blacker it became
An enshrouding grey season
A mist of grave-flowers in a dusk of swords

Lithium Carbonate

I do not like you; I do not like your power
It is not as if you can power my watch
Or turn my clock mind back to mimic your dull

White, so I pour water on you; my brain like a shaking wet cat
Off, off ghastly sticky thing you make me retch
Heaving up my milky opaque mind like a blunt knife – it

Is only good for an angry stab at my arm whilst drunk anyway
It needs stitches. Stitches, stitches? Something must be sewn up
Otherwise things will fall out and drop behind the couch or 'neath

My bed. Oh lost it is lost, all is lost. Help me doctor, help me safe
Clinic. Draw my blood and check my levels. Are they alright? Are
They fine? Exhale then, all is cool you say! Hooray, hooray, in your

Book, pencil me in okay.
Next Thursday I'll be:
A lot more blunt
A lot less shiny!

Burrs

Wandering around inside myself
Secrets appear – drifting passengers of hush
Fingers to their lips and stilted
Something in my blood simmers and renders my brain
a fidgety occupant of my skull

Feeling like Plath's tulips
I bunch myself into each day
In beats, beats
Heartbeats, the heart contracts
You'd think everything I see
would be all red, but

Instead, the world I see is yellow
Like an old photograph
It is all ice to me
My hands too – sculptured ice, splitting light
into hundreds of pieces, like birds coming home
a fog of wings settling on grey stonework

In my First House, the Lord of the Oceans resides
The master magician mystifying the masses
Neptune has a soul, yet it borrows mine too
It is the base of a gas flame, all blue
And its blue face makes me itch
An itch vague and insatiable

I would like to touch dark matter
I am sure it feels like wasted stars
Countless buttons to seal my darkness –
Burrs: you little devil-smiles!
Prickle and scratch
my naked arms.

Concentricity

The mirror of the sky's grey face shatters
illusions of last night; they splinter into dark alleyways
crunching, my boots choke back tears of wet streets
and the last grains of hope become trapped in their grooves

It is incomprehensible to a tree-skewered riverbank:
my heart blooming like an Azalea through my damp skin
it is neither lead nor stone, yet it weighs a ton of wind through my hair
and cerulean eyes are electric with despair

Unravel the stairs, under falling plaster
from it all I cannot make new shapes
I can only turn my face slowly like a sunflower
to the east, where the sun forgot to rise.

Sheath

Sheath
disturbance in the airwaves
Sheath
something old, something new
Sheath
your scar smiles at me
Sheath
snuggle in your tunnel
Sheath
hunger snaps ribs

Sheath, a cocoon –

world I spin *you* into
a garment of black cotton.

The Offering (under Thunderwood skies)

You have kept your heart hidden
like a coven in the woods.
The moon, too, shrouds itself in drapes
of icy rain darts. The night is an Argus
its starry spies are wise,
they peruse my open dream-book
when I'm naked at the altar
bound with ropes
of self-sacrifice.
Am I not the smoke of devotion unwinding
drifting up and out to the one I love?

A Sunday Afternoon

Remember that Sunday afternoon?
Cajun calamari for lunch at The Brass Bell and then
We drove all the way down to Cape Point on a whim
I had made you that Cat Stevens CD with all your favourites
His voice trailing from the open windows, our fights and tensions
Left behind for the day, replaced by your singing and my laughing
The gates of the reserve were already closed by the time we got there
"It's okay," we agreed. "The drive was lovely enough."
The cliffs stepped out of the last spring sunlight into the ocean
as we headed back, your one hand on the wheel, and the other
searching for mine. Making light conversation along the way, we were keen
to save the mood. "Would you like me to stay the night?"
you asked tentatively as we got back to my place.

It's funny, I'll always fondly remember us buying tomatoes
at eight o'clock on a spring Sunday evening.

Softly, softly

For Slinky

It makes me smile
The way sunflowers turn towards you
How they wish to hold you!
And even rain that falls gently
It, too, is envious of you:
Delicate, elegant
Matched perhaps only by the stars.

And do you know
That your skin whispers to me
That even air motes stand aside for us?
So carefully, mysteriously, as if by magic
And all these infinite spaces closing fast
As I tumble
White-hot through the corridors of your heart
Towards the light of your soul.

And, I Will

from the bittersweet earth
of my longing

every night,
like a flower that
cannot stop opening,

nail myself to a cross

And, I will

hand you a blade
I *will* you to slice me open
I *want* you to see
how scarlet I am for you.

On Saying Goodbye

You want to drop the coal; because it burns
You want to drop the bomb; because its blast
is beautiful and apocalyptic, it cleanses –

The heat has split the hurt evenly between us

An eclipse – the now dead centre of flames in which
We had loved
So drop it, drop it, drop it, now
we drop it
From a height that only comets can relate to

Are you now walking on the doused coals as I do?
Are you picking through the charred remains as I do?

Our moon had long been waning, yet

Still, I breathe in
Your every breathing out.

Walls

A heart able to hallucinate flowers
Their petals – I lay them down
So I may remember my way
Maybe, once again, they would become something
Like a deck of cards I could shuffle, then deal
With some luck, a Last Gamble.

But…
Here and now, I love and marvel at my walls
So rough to my touch, so sturdy for the coming winter
I see old tears like dew have dried to diamonds on the parapet

And while I was at it

I thought I should brick up the door I'd left for you
Though it's true, I cannot keep the ghosts at bay
They were always this side of my spine anyway
I feel them reach out from glances in a hand-held mirror

Diamonds: I keep them in a box named Seasons
Buried far below the foundation
A pure white coffin, a fine resting place
And beneath the lid – memories a restless scent and still warm whispers.

And though the streets of my inner Berlin seam endlessly through me
I am secure, for now – no checkpoints through which the outside can pass
These walls: someday maybe someone offers me
A hammer and reasons
They may just come down with the dust of a thousand mile journey
At the break of dawn like a tumbling Jericho.

Husk

Whipped into a corner by some gust
Torn at the edges, far below

A window, stains of dried rain like copper
A place where ragged nails taste like an obituary

A track to nowhere, lay this swan down over the sleepers
Gently does it, the palms

of summer have offered powdered bones
into the hum of power line days

Let me have your clamorous stare; the red eye
of this ember hisses into past womb-waters

I am diaphanous, a web, or just an empty

Shell.

Detonation Alley

Treacherous years!
And thirty-three of them since
Some god unkilled me
Tore me from safe womb waters
And put knives into my side
Put glass into my feet
And with a torsion of high-tensile wires for veins
Sent me on my way, wrawling against the world.

Burnt, crushed, skewered or hanged
Drawn and quartered –
Nevertheless,
I have an immense heart
Which is drowning
In itself
See the fury, the passion that turns it red
To white.

A shooting star has such a distance to travel!
Before it burns itself out or crashes to the ground
What a lasting impact I shall make
Seen by the world, water
Will fill it, water, water - safe and sound

In up to my neck
I am coy with lit fuse in hand –
a ticking man, these
Shrapnel fragments that blast through alleys.

Birthday

Extrication –
Forceps bloody the body of innocence
Slipping on the sludge of inertia, then

Something heaves violently
Rib-cracking lung-burst
From the expansion of a single breath

Turns flying shards of panic into shrapnel
Turns my heart an alien hue, spatter
The damaged loves, bullet-riddled by old hurts

Silent tears: a world rimmed red
But I stand. Stand against the wind
Gritting my teeth against its shriek, as

It scythes straight through me
But still I stand. Rooted, rooted as a tree
I am old, older.

Add another ring.

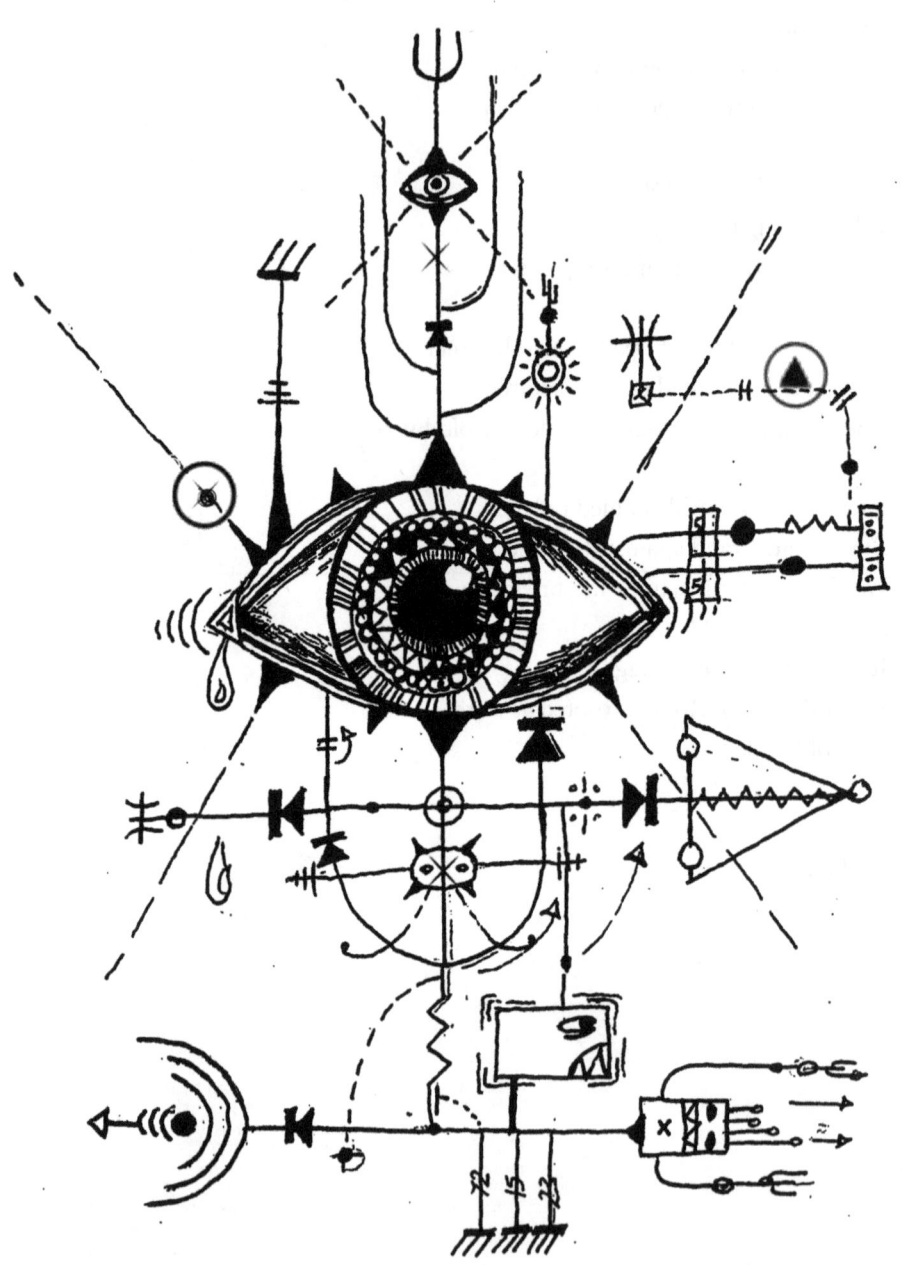

Shock, decoded

Blink stare blink
A red eye means I'm on standby
Glow, cathode-ray, decode
The equation of this laceration
And a mind of salt, a mouth of sand
Blink stare blink
In a white-out of the bends
The hard water of micro frames:
Frame by frame they told me
That you're dead, please
Don't tell me
that
you're
dead.

Scattering Your Ashes at Kalk Bay

For J.F.P

I am heavy over the rocky outcrop for the weight of my heart
But you are light in my palm and through my fingers
As though you've filtered like time through an hourglass
Lighter, now, than even the mild winter air, sky and sea
That had called us out today to blend you with it.

And what gifts has the fire left for the blue?
Your bones are powdered, mine are broken
A bag of stars and shells to replace a body

And from my hand I seem to have tethered a spirit
To Heaven's cradle:
A scatter of distances from womb to horizon

A grief beads and drips into a rock pool at my feet –
I feel I have lost a jewel among the sea-fern and abalone;
Here we keep our silence close to our chests,
Burrowing deep within us, as heavy as God;
But you -

You are light now, lighter than even the song
"Time After Time"
Wisping from the Harbour House restaurant
As we clamber in our armour, back up
To the path yellowed by the flowering Freesias.

About the Author

Nick Purdon was born in 1976 in East London in the Eastern Cape province of South Africa. After a few moves around the country, his family settled in the Western Cape city of Cape Town in 1981 where he has lived since. Nick began writing poetry seriously at the age of 27, though he had been writing on and off since his teenage years. Along with various projects with his sister in web and graphic design and visual art, he intends to follow this collection up with more poetry in the future, as well as a collection of short stories and childrens stories. He is also active in the field of addiction counseling and working on a full-length book detailing his own addiction experiences.

Introducing the World Voices Series

This series highlights the best English-language autobiography, fiction, and poetry of diverse voices from Africa, Asia, the Caribbean, and South America.

Because All Is Not Lost: Verse on Grief
By Sweta Srivastava Vikram

Kaleidoscope: An Asian Journey with Colors.
By Sweta Srivastava Vikram

The Blue Fairy and other tales of transcendence
By Ernest Dempsey

Iraq Through a Bullet Hole: A Civilian Wikileaks
by Issam Jameel

The Road-Shaped Heart
by Nick Purdon

from Modern History Press
http://www.modernhistorypress.com/world-voices/

www.ingramcontent.com/pod-product-compliance
Lightning Source LLC
Chambersburg PA
CBHW061307040426
42444CB00010B/2549